Useful Machines
# Levers

Chris Oxlade

Heinemann Library
Chicago, Illinois

Originated by Ambassador Litho Ltd.
Printed and bound in China by South China Printing Company

07 06 05 04 03
10 9 8 7 6 5 4 3 2 1

**Library of Congress Cataloging-in-Publication Data**
Oxlade, Chris.
  Levers / Chris Oxlade.
     v. cm. -- (Useful machines)
Includes bibliographical references and index.
Contents: What is a lever? -- What does a lever do? -- How does a lever work? -- Loads and efforts -- Levers together -- Pivots at the end -- More levers -- Levers for cutting -- Levers for turning -- Levers for digging -- Working levers -- Levers for control -- Amazing lever facts.
  ISBN 1-4034-3662-2 (lib. bdg.) -- ISBN 1-4034-3677-0 (pbk.)
  1. Levers--Juvenile literature. 2. Lifting and carrying--Juvenile literature. [1. Levers.] I. Title. II. Series.
  TJ147.O84 2003
  621.8--dc21
                                         2003003786
**Acknowledgments**
The author and publisher are grateful to the following for permission to reproduce copyright material:
pp. 4, 9, 10, 11, 12, 17, 19, 20, 22, 26 Pete Morris; p. 5 Barry Lewis/Corbis; p. 6 Garden Picture Library/Lamontagne; pp. 7, 13, 16 Trevor Clifford; pp. 8, 15, 25 Alamy Images; p. 14 Anthony Blake Photo Library; p. 18 Royalty-Free/Corbis; p. 21 H. Rogers/Trip; p. 23 Robert Maass/Corbis; p. 24 Construction Photography; p. 27 Onne Van Der Wal/Corbis; p. 29 Craig Lovell/Corbis.

Cover photograph by Lester Lefkowitz/Corbis.

Every effort has been made to contact copyright holders of any material reproduced in this book. Any omissions will be rectified in subsequent printings if notice is given to the publisher.

Some words are shown in bold, **like this.** You can find out what they mean by looking in the glossary.

Useful Machines
# Levers
Chris Oxlade

Heinemann Library
Chicago, Illinois

Originated by Ambassador Litho Ltd.
Printed and bound in China by South China Printing Company

07 06 05 04 03
10 9 8 7 6 5 4 3 2 1

**Library of Congress Cataloging-in-Publication Data**
Oxlade, Chris.
  Levers / Chris Oxlade.
      v. cm. --  (Useful machines)
Includes bibliographical references and index.
Contents: What is a lever? -- What does a lever do? -- How does a lever work? -- Loads and efforts -- Levers together -- Pivots at the end -- More levers -- Levers for cutting -- Levers for turning -- Levers for digging -- Working levers -- Levers for control -- Amazing lever facts.
  ISBN 1-4034-3662-2 (lib. bdg.) -- ISBN 1-4034-3677-0 (pbk.)
  1.  Levers--Juvenile literature. 2.  Lifting and carrying--Juvenile literature. [1. Levers.]  I. Title. II. Series.
  TJ147.O84 2003
  621.8--dc21

                              2003003786
**Acknowledgments**
The author and publisher are grateful to the following for permission to reproduce copyright material:
pp. 4, 9, 10, 11, 12, 17, 19, 20, 22, 26 Pete Morris; p. 5 Barry Lewis/Corbis; p. 6 Garden Picture Library/Lamontagne; pp. 7, 13, 16 Trevor Clifford; pp. 8, 15, 25 Alamy Images; p. 14 Anthony Blake Photo Library; p. 18 Royalty-Free/Corbis; p. 21 H. Rogers/Trip; p. 23 Robert Maass/Corbis; p. 24 Construction Photography; p. 27 Onne Van Der Wal/Corbis; p. 29 Craig Lovell/Corbis.

Cover photograph by Lester Lefkowitz/Corbis.

Every effort has been made to contact copyright holders of any material reproduced in this book. Any omissions will be rectified in subsequent printings if notice is given to the publisher.

Some words are shown in bold, **like this.** You can find out what they mean by looking in the glossary.

# Contents

What Is a Lever? . . . . . . . . . . . . . . . . . .4

What Does a Lever Do? . . . . . . . . . . .6

Parts of a Lever . . . . . . . . . . . . . . . . .8

How Does a Lever Work? . . . . . . . .10

Fulcrum in Between . . . . . . . . . . . . .12

Load in Between . . . . . . . . . . . . . . .14

Force in Between . . . . . . . . . . . . . .16

Levers for Cutting . . . . . . . . . . . . . .18

Levers for Turning . . . . . . . . . . . . .20

Working Levers . . . . . . . . . . . . . . . .22

Levers for Digging . . . . . . . . . . . . .24

Levers in Control . . . . . . . . . . . . . .26

Amazing Lever Facts . . . . . . . . . . . .28

Glossary . . . . . . . . . . . . . . . . . . . . .30

More Books to Read . . . . . . . . . . . .32

Index . . . . . . . . . . . . . . . . . . . . . . .32

# What Is a Lever?

lever

A machine makes our lives easier by helping us do things. Machines are made up of **simple machines** that work together. This simple machine is called a lever.

A lever is a very useful machine. These people are using levers to lift a heavy log. Without the levers, it would be very hard to move the log.

# What Does a Lever Do?

A lever makes a **pull** or a **push.** This pitchfork is a lever. When you pull back on the handle, the soil gets pushed forward.

pulling back on handle

soil moving forward

Levers can also be used to squash, grip, and cut things. The handles of this nutcracker are levers. When you press them together, the nut breaks open.

# Parts of a Lever

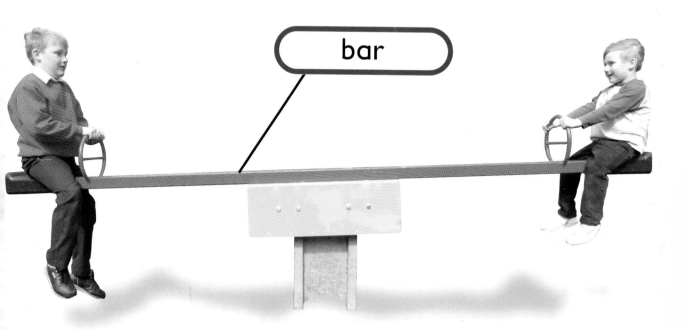

bar

Many levers have just two parts. One of them is a strong rod or a bar. A seesaw is a lever. It has a strong bar made of wood or metal.

fulcrum

Each lever also has a **fulcrum.** The fulcrum is the place where a lever is **attached** or **balanced** so it can move. The fulcrum on a seesaw is at the middle of the bar.

# How Does a Lever Work?

load

People often use levers to lift objects. The weight of the object **pushes** down on the lever. This is called the **load.** Here, the load is the weight of the **drain** cover.

force

A person pushes or **pulls** on a lever to make it move. This push or pull is called **force.** Here, the man pushes down on the bar. This push will lift the drain cover.

# Fulcrum in Between

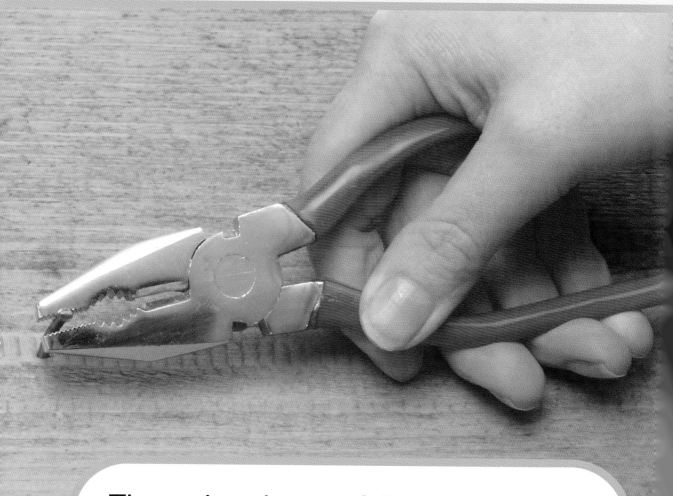

These pliers have a **fulcrum** between the **force** and the **load. Pushing** the handles makes the jaws move together. They grip the nail.

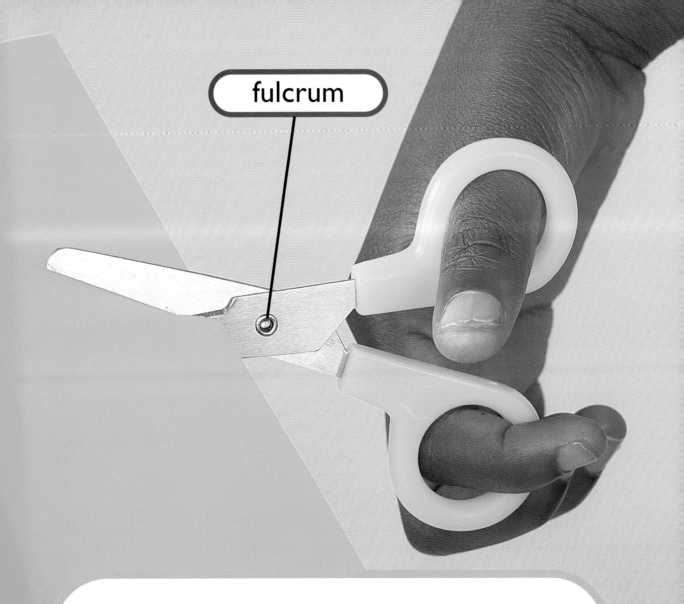

fulcrum

A pair of scissors has two levers with a fulcrum in the middle. Squeezing the handles makes the **blades** come together. The blades cut the paper.

# Load in Between

This garlic press has the **load** between the **fulcrum** and the **force.** Because the garlic is near the fulcrum, the **push** on the garlic is very strong. It is squashed easily.

A wheelbarrow is also a lever. The wheel is the fulcrum. The objects in the wheelbarrow are the load. This big lever makes it easier to lift the load.

# Force in Between

Some levers have the **force** between the **fulcrum** and the **load.** Tweezers make the force smaller so you do not hurt yourself.

The top of this stapler is a lever. The fulcrum is **attached** to the stapler's base. When you press on the stapler, it **pushes** a staple through the paper.

# Levers for Cutting

This is a paper cutter. The handle and **blade** are a long lever. The lever makes it easy to cut many sheets of paper at the same time.

Garden shears have two levers **joined** by a **fulcrum. Pushing** the handles together moves the blades together. They slice through branches easily.

# Levers for Turning

Levers also help to turn things. A wrench is a lever. You use it to tighten or loosen a **nut** or **bolt. Pulling** or **pushing** on the wrench's handle makes the nut or bolt turn.

A long lever makes it easier to turn a nut or bolt. This is a tire iron for tightening or loosening the nuts on a car wheel. It has a long handle.

# Working Levers

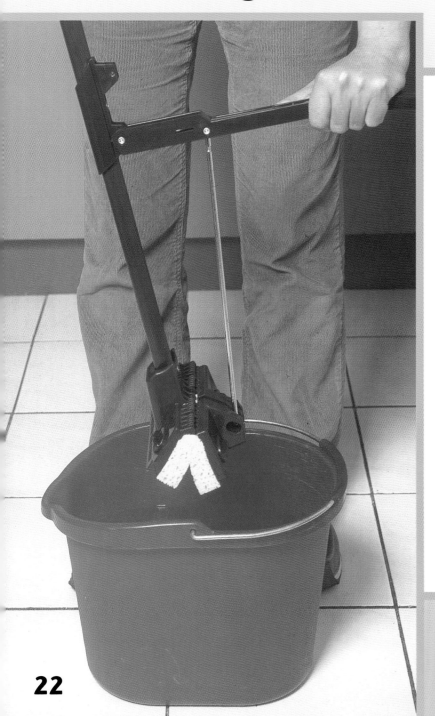

A lever can be part of another machine. This floor mop has a lever on its handle. The lever is used to squeeze the sponge. This squeezes out the dirty water.

This is a water pump. It pumps drinking water from deep underground. The long handle is a lever. This lever makes it easier to work the pump.

# Levers for Digging

Power shovels have many levers. One lever is on the end of the power shovel's arm. It can dig holes and lift heavy objects.

hydraulic
cylinder

The levers on the power shovel's arm need very strong **pushes** and **pulls** to make them move. Powerful **hydraulic cylinders** do the pushing and pulling.

# Levers in Control

Levers are often used to control machines. A bicycle has levers on the handlebar. When you **pull** the brake levers, rubber blocks press against the wheels. This slows the bicycle down.

You **steer** a sailboat with a **tiller.**
The tiller is a lever. **Pushing** and pulling
on the tiller moves a flat piece of wood
in the water. This is called the rudder.
The rudder makes the boat turn.

# Amazing Lever Facts

- The lower part of your arm works just like a lever. Your elbow is the **fulcrum,** and your **muscles push** and **pull.**
- The lever is one of the oldest machines in the world. It was invented thousands of years ago.
- The long ladder on top of a fire engine is a lever. The fulcrum is on the bottom of the ladder.
- There are more than 250 levers in a piano.
- In each of your ears there are three small bones that work like levers. They help you hear sounds.

Some bridges are made of two huge levers. The sides of the bridge lift to let ships pass underneath. Bridges like this are called bascule bridges.

# Glossary

**attach**   fasten or join together

**balance**   keep something steady so that it does not fall over

**blade**   narrow strip of metal with a sharp edge

**bolt**   rod with a screw thread around the outside

**drain**   pipe that carries wastewater away

**force**   push or pull

**fulcrum**   place on a lever where it is attached or balanced. The lever moves around the fulcrum.

**hydraulic cylinder**   machine that uses water or oil under pressure to make pushes and pulls

**join**   put two or more things together

**load** thing that you are trying to lift, move, or squash

**muscle** part of the body used for movement, such as walking or lifting

**nut** four- or six-sided object with a hole in the middle and a screw thread inside

**pull** move something closer to you

**push** move something away from you

**simple machine** machine with no moving parts

**steer** make a vehicle or a boat change direction

**tiller** bar that a sailor pushes and pulls to steer a small boat

# More Books to Read

Douglas, Lloyd G. *What Is a Lever?* Danbury, Conn.:
   Scholastic Library Publishing, 2002.
Frost, Helen. *What Are Levers?* Minnetonka, Minn.:
   Capstone Press, 2001.
Welsbacher, Anne. *Levers.* Minnetonka, Minn.:
   Capstone Press, 2000.

# Index

body levers  28
controlling machines  26–27
cutting  7, 13, 18–19
digging  24–25
force  11, 12, 14, 16
fulcrum  9, 12, 13, 14, 15, 16,
   17, 19, 28
gripping  7, 12
lifting  5, 10, 11
load  10, 12, 14, 15, 16

machines  4, 5, 22,
   26, 28
pulling and pushing  6, 10,
   11, 12, 13, 14, 17, 19, 20,
   25, 26, 27, 28
pump  23
rods and bars  8, 9, 11
seesaw  8, 9
squashing  7, 14, 22
turning  20–21